Classics
Romantics · Moderns

SOLOS FOR THE INTERMEDIATE PIANIST
Compiled and Edited by Paul Sheftel

D1608295

CARL FISCHER®
65 Bleecker Street, New York, NY 10012

ATF102

ISBN 0-8258-0344-6

Table of Contents

About this book...

For any one who likes the "desert island" game as much as I do — what books, music, records, toys, food, etc. would you want with you if you were stranded on a deserted island?—compiling an anthology is a most challenging and yet appealing task. It was indeed in the "desert island" spirit that I set out assembling this collection; asking myself which piano pieces would I choose were I only to include my all time favorites, either from my experience as a student or as a teacher.

But why, some may ask, another anthology with many of the very familiar pieces which are already included elsewhere? To this I can only answer: because these are the classic pieces which are the heritage of every piano student. No compilation which purports to present a cross-section of piano literature could fail to include them.

My first consideration, then, was to try to include the most interesting and appealing examples from the "student literature" and while these books should be welcomed by all lovers of piano music they are primarily intended for the piano student.

Editing has deliberately been done with a light touch. In the cases of the Baroque and Classical examples for which there are few or no original indications, some musical suggestions have been provided; sparingly in some instances, in others, not at all. These edited examples are meant to serve as guidelines for those which are unedited, where students and teachers can exercise their own judgement regarding such matters as tempo, touch and dynamics. I have used Urtext sources whenever possible.

Fingerings have also been provided as sparingly as possible, in most instances only to indicate a change of position. Passages which recur are not fingered, thus obliging the student to recognize the return of a previously given passage, and to finger it accordingly. Fingering is, of course, very personal and students and teachers are always urged to explore alternative fingering possibilities.

The pieces within a given volume are, generally, at a comparable level of difficulty. *Beginning Piano Solos* presents the more elementary level, *More Classics • Romantics • Moderns* the most advanced, while *Classics • Romantics • Moderns* bridges the two levels. Grading, however, can be misleading since seemingly simple pieces can often present obstacles for some students, while so-called advanced pieces often prove to be surprisingly manageable. These classifications, therefore, should only be taken as general guidelines.

It will be noted that certain composers are better represented than others. This apparent imbalance results from the obvious fact that some composers have been more prolific than others in writing inspired short piano pieces of only moderate difficulty.

In closing, the editor hopes that the many hours spent with these books may be rewarding ones to each of you and that if you should ever get to a "desert island" you may well remember to bring this repertoire with you.

Paul Sheftel

Fanfare
(Trumpet Tune)

HENRY PURCELL
(1658-1695)

Les Coucous

(The Cuckoos)

FRANÇOIS COUPERIN
(1668-1733)

Impertinence

GEORGE FRIDERIC HANDEL
(1685-1759)

Copyright © 1984 by Carl Fischer, Inc.

8

Prelude

GEORGE FRIDERIC HANDEL
(1685-1759)

Minuet

GEORGE FRIDERIC HANDEL
(1685-1759)

Copyright © 1984 by Carl Fischer, Inc.

Jigg

GEORGE FRIDERIC HANDEL
(1685-1759)

Aria

GEORGE FRIDERIC HANDEL
(1685-1759)

ATF102

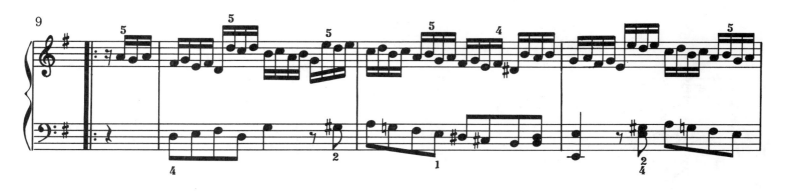

Sarabande

GEORGE FRIDERIC HANDEL
(1685-1759)

Variation I

Minuet

JOHANN SEBASTIAN BACH
(1685-1750)

Prelude

JOHANN SEBASTIAN BACH, BWV 939
(1685-1750)

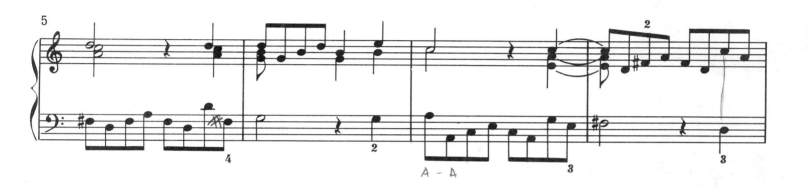

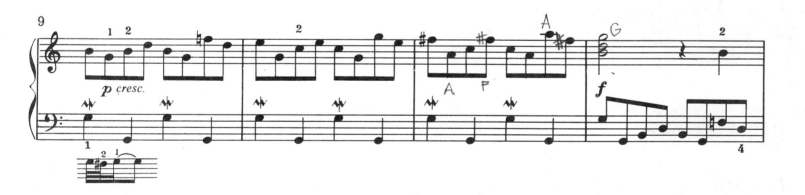

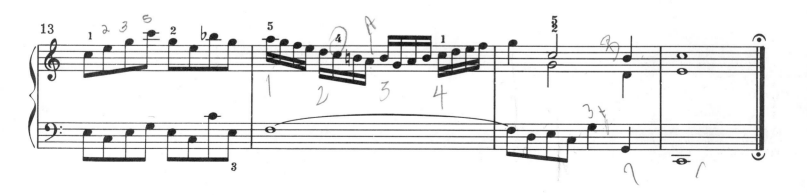

Bourrée

From *Suite in E Minor*

JOHANN SEBASTIAN BACH, BWV 996
(1685-1750)

Minuet

DOMENICO SCARLATTI, K.83b; L.S.31
(1685-1757)

Aria

DOMENICO SCARLATTI, K.32; L.423
(1685-1757)

Allegro

WILHELM FRIEDEMANN BACH
(1710-1784)

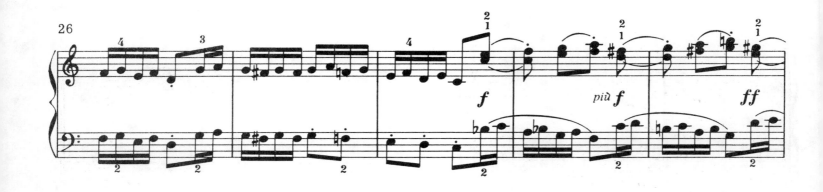

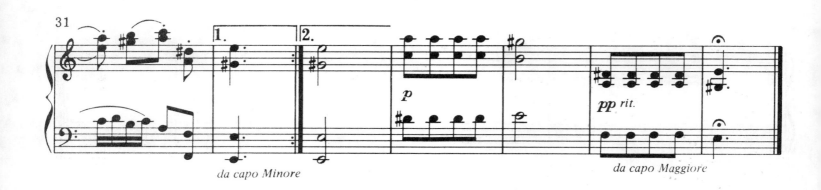

da capo Minore

da capo Maggiore

Pastorale

CARL PHILIPP EMANUEL BACH
(1714-1788)

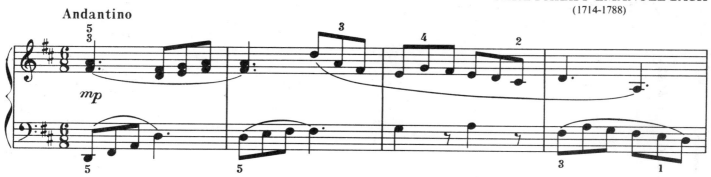

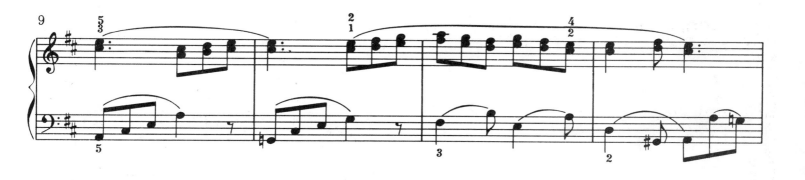

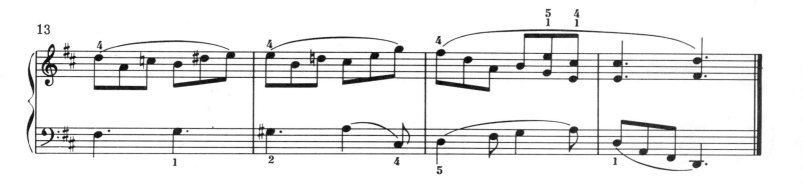

Allegro

CARL PHILIPP EMANUEL BACH
(1714-1788)

Fantasia

CARL PHILIPP EMANUEL BACH
(1714-1788)

ATF102

Solfeggio

CARL PHILIPP EMANUEL BACH
(1714-1788)

29

ATF102

Fantasia

CARL PHILIPP EMANUEL BACH
(1714-1788)

Allegro assai

Allegro

LEOPOLD MOZART
(1719-1787)

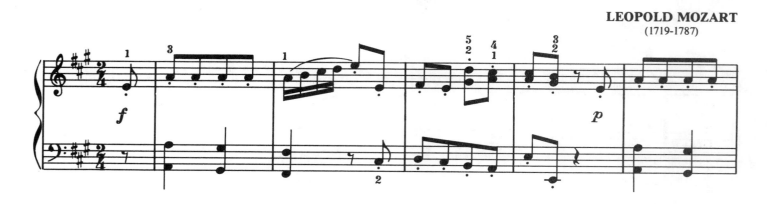

Minuet

FRANZ JOSEPH HAYDN
(1732-1809)

Copyright © 1984 by Carl Fischer, Inc.

Allegro

FRANZ JOSEPH HAYDN, Hob.III: 73/4
(1732-1809)

Vivace

FRANZ JOSEPH HAYDN
(1732-1809)

37

ATF102

D.C. al Fine

ATF102

Allegro

FRANZ JOSEPH HAYDN
(1732-1809)

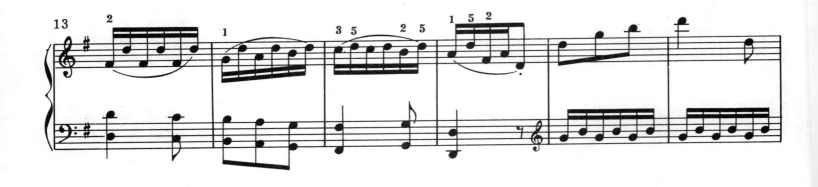

Sonatina

MUZIO CLEMENTI, Op. 36, No. 1
(1752-1832)

42

44

Minuet

WOLFGANG AMADEUS MOZART
(1756-1791)

Presto
from *The London Notebook*

WOLFGANG AMADEUS MOZART, K.15
(1756-1791)

Minuet

LUDWIG van BEETHOVEN, K.WoO 10, No. 1
(1770-1827)

Fine

Menuet da Capo

Bagatelle

LUDWIG van BEETHOVEN, Op. 119, No. 9
(1770-1827)

Country Dance

LUDWIG van BEETHOVEN
(1770-1827)

Copyright © 1984 by Carl Fischer, Inc.

Country Dance

LUDWIG van BEETHOVEN
(1770-1827)

German Dance

LUDWIG van BEETHOVEN
(1770-1827)

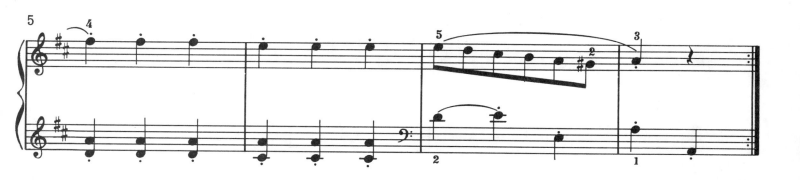

Minuet

LUDWIG van BEETHOVEN
(1770-1827)

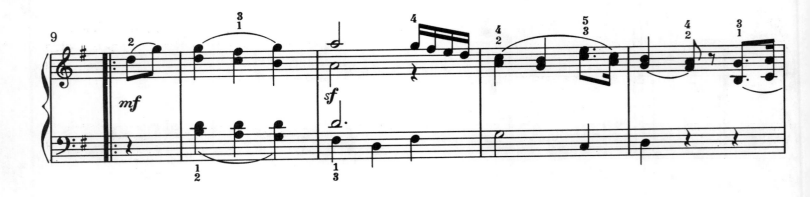

17 Trio

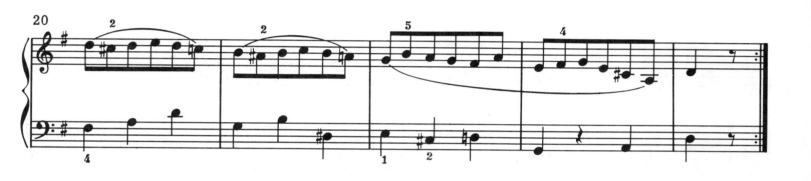

20

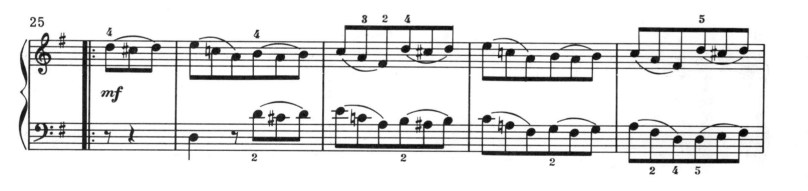

25 *mf*

29

Menuet da Capo

Happy and Sad

(Lustig und Traurig)

LUDWIG van BEETHOVEN, Op. WoO 54
(1770–1827)

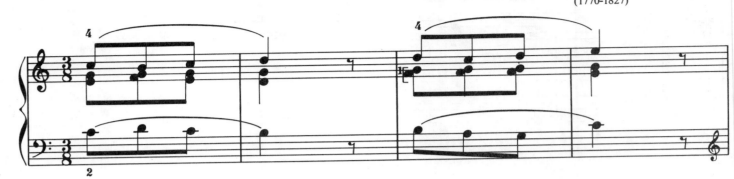

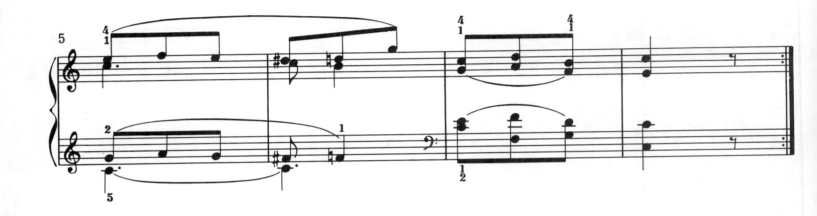

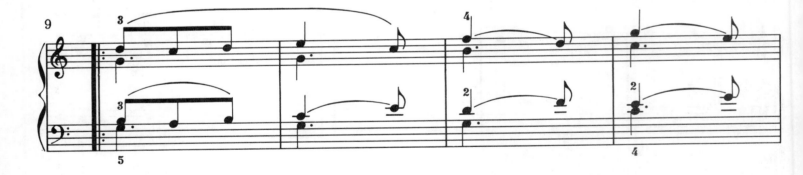

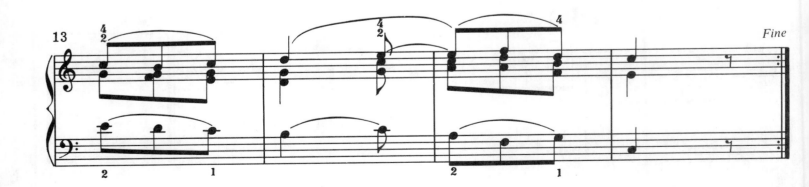

minore

D.C.

Sonatina

LUDWIG van BEETHOVEN, Op. Anh. 5, No. 1
(1770-1827)

60

Romanze

ATF102

Sonatina

LUDWIG van BEETHOVEN, Op. Anh. 5 , No. 2
(1770-1827)

ATF102

Allemande

CARL MARIA von WEBER, Op. 4, No. 2
(1786-1826)

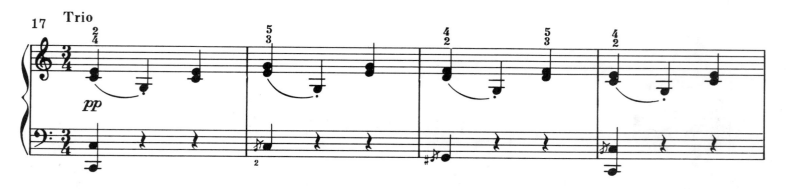

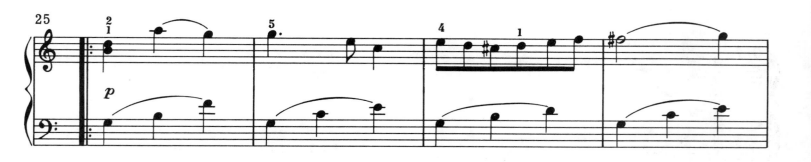

D.C. al Fine

ATF102

Scherzo

CARL MARIA von WEBER
(1786-1826)

D.C. al Fine

Study

CARL CZERNY, Op. 821, No. 1
(1791-1857)

Ecossaise

FRANZ SCHUBERT, Op. 33, No. 1
(1797-1828)

Ecossaise

FRANZ SCHUBERT, Op. 33, No. 2
(1797-1828)

ATF102

Copyright © 1984 by Carl Fischer, Inc.

Waltz

from *12 Grätzer Walzer*

FRANZ SCHUBERT, Op. 91a, No. 9
(1797-1828)

Waltz

FRANZ SCHUBERT, Op. 18, No. 5
(1797-1828)

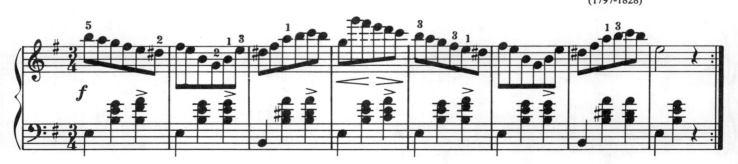

Waltz

FRANZ SCHUBERT, Op. 18a, No. 6
(1797-1828)

ATF102

Five German Dances
called *Ländler*

FRANZ SCHUBERT, D.366
(1797-1828)

The Chase
(La Chasse)

FRIEDRICH BURGMÜLLER, Op. 100, No. 9
(1806-1874)

The Farewell
(L'Adieu)

FRIEDRICH BURGMÜLLER, Op. 100, No. 12
(1806-1874)

Ballade

FRIEDRICH BURGMÜLLER, Op. 100, No. 15
(1806-1874)

Andante
from *6 Children's Pieces*

FELIX MENDELSSOHN-BARTHOLDY, Op. 72, No. 5
(1809-1847)

Little Hunting Song

(Jägerliedchen)

from *Album for the Young*

ROBERT SCHUMANN, Op. 68, No. 7
(1810-1856)

The Happy Farmer
(Fröhlicher Landmann)
from *Album for the Young*

ROBERT SCHUMANN, Op. 68, No. 10
(1810-1856)

Animato e grazioso

Sicilian

(Sizilianisch)

from *Album for the Young*

ROBERT SCHUMANN, Op. 68, No. 11
(1810-1856)

Da capo al fine senza repetizione

The Reaper's Song
(Schnitterliedchen)
from *Album for the Young*

ROBERT SCHUMANN, Op. 68, No. 18
(1810-1856)

Avalanche

STEPHEN HELLER, Op. 45, No. 2
(1813-1888)

Vivace

STEPHEN HELLER, Op. 46, No. 7
(1813-1888)

Allegretto

STEPHEN HELLER, Op. 47, No. 3
(1813-1888)

Allegretto con moto

Allegretto

STEPHEN HELLER, Op. 47, No. 5
(1813-1888)

Allegretto poco agitato ♩ = 126

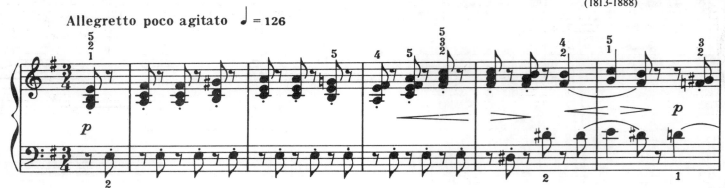

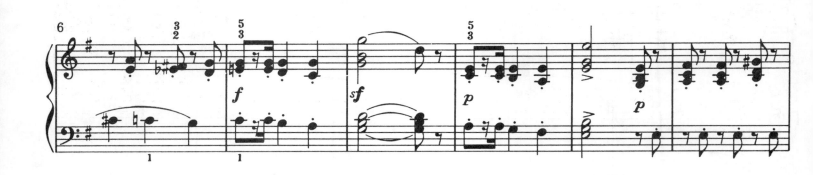

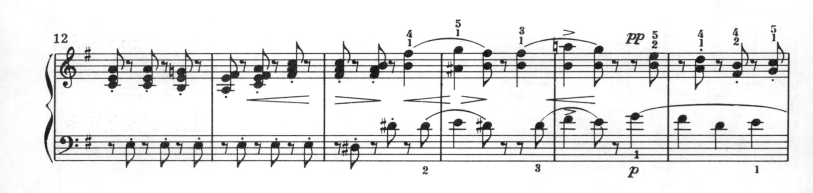

Vivace

STEPHEN HELLER, Op. 47, No. 7
(1813-1888)

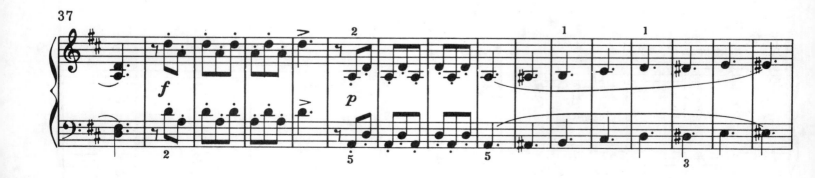

Vivace

STEPHEN HELLER, Op. 47, No. 18
(1813-1888)

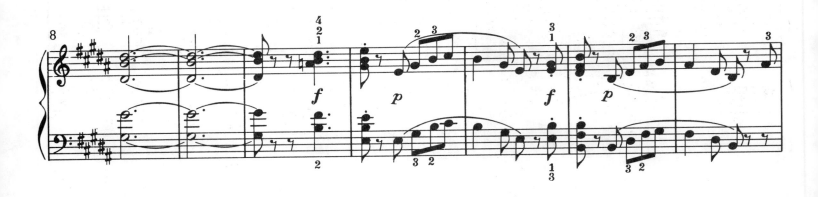

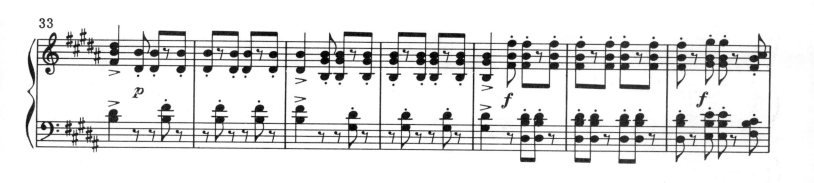

Spinning Song

ALBERT ELLMENREICH, Op. 14, No. 4
(1816-1905)

Italian Song

from *Album for the Young*

PETER ILYICH TCHAIKOVSKY, Op. 39, No. 15
(1840-1893)

Old French Song

from *Album for the Young*

PETER ILYICH TCHAIKOVSKY, Op. 39, No. 16
(1840-1893)

German Song

from *Album for the Young*

PETER ILYICH TCHAIKOVSKY, Op. 39, No. 17

(1840-1893)

A Winter Morning

from *Album for the Young*

PETER ILYICH TCHAIKOVSKY, Op. 39, No. 2
(1840-1893)

Waltz

from *Album for the Young*

PETER ILYICH TCHAIKOVSKY, Op. 39, No. 8
(1840-1893)

Copyright © 1984 by Carl Fischer, Inc.

Mazurka
from *Album for the Young*

PETER ILYICH TCHAIKOVSKY, Op. 39, No. 10
(1840-1893)

Waltz

"Vals" from *Lyric Pieces,* Book I

EDVARD GRIEG, Op. 12, No. 2
(1843-1907)

114

ATF102

Elfin-Dance
"Aelfedans" from *Lyric Pieces,* Book I

EDVARD GRIEG, Op. 38, No. 4
(1843-1907)

Molto allegro e sempre staccato

Album Leaf

"Albumblad" from *Lyric Pieces*, Book I

EDVARD GRIEG, Op. 68, No. 1
(1843-1907)

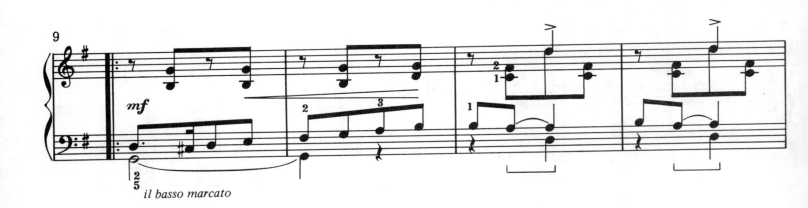

Folksong

"Folkevise" from *Lyric Pieces,* Book II

EDVARD GRIEG, Op. 38, No. 2
(1843-1907)

Sailor's Song

"Matrosernes opsang" from *Lyric Pieces,* Book IX

EDVARD GRIEG, Op. 68, No. 1
(1843-1907)

Allegro vivace e marcato

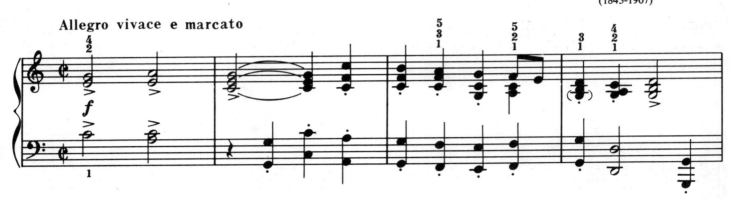

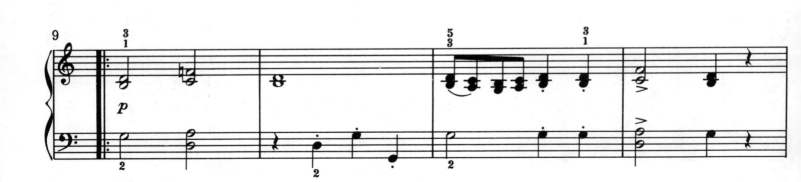

Children's Game

No. 8 from *For Children*, Vol. 1

BÉLA BARTÓK
(1881-1945)

Allegro

No. 12 from *For Children*, Vol. 1

BÉLA BARTÓK
(1881-1945)

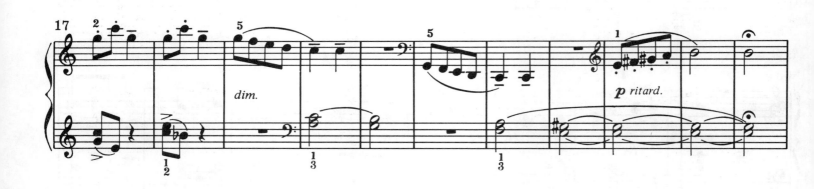

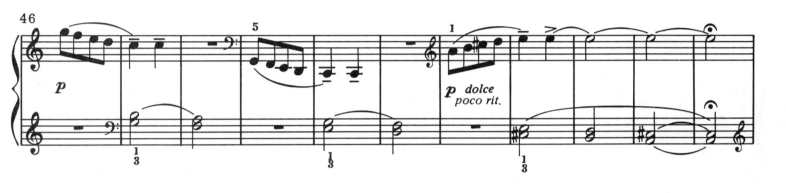

Sailor's Dance

No. 21 from *For Children,* Vol. 1

BÉLA BARTÓK
(1881-1945)

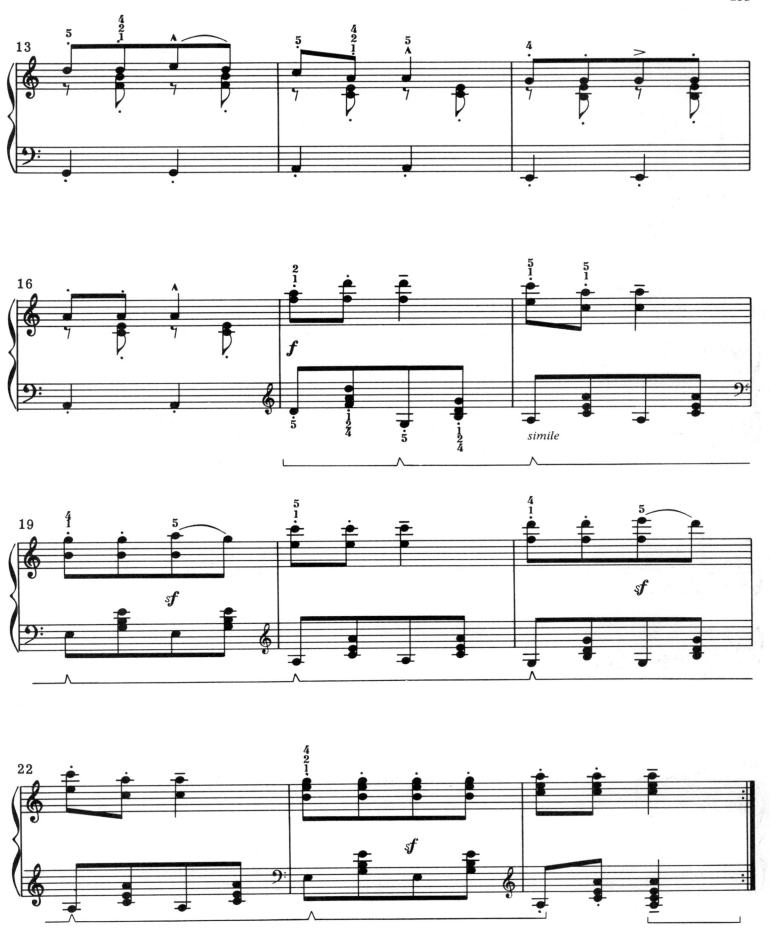

Round Dance

No. 17 from *For Children*, Vol. 1

BÉLA BARTÓK
(1881-1945)

Round Dance I

No. 6 from *For Children*, Vol. 2

BÉLA BARTÓK
(1881-1945)

Fiddlin' Joe

from *Tintypes*

DOUGLAS MOORE
(1893-1969)

Dance of the Warriors

(after an ancient northern tune)

HOWARD HANSON
(1896-1981)

ATF102

March

ROGER SESSIONS
(1896-1985)

The Irishman Dances

HENRY COWELL
(1897-1965)

Sunday Afternoon Music

AARON COPLAND
(1900-1990)

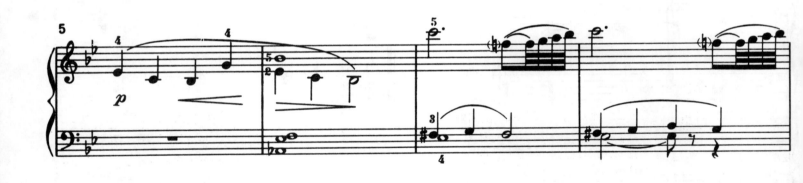

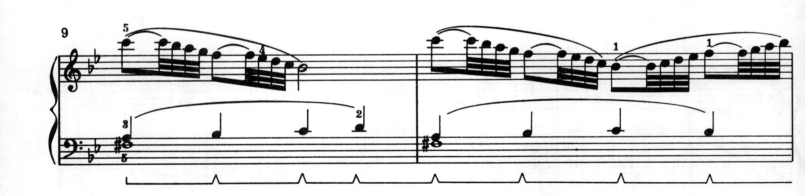

11

simile

17

14

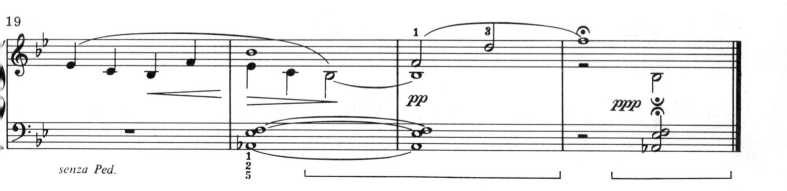

19

senza Ped.

_pp_

ppp

Selected Music for Piano from the
CARL FISCHER MUSIC LIBRARY

Intermediate Level Piano Books by Paul Sheftel

Cat. No. O5318

Cat. No. O5317

Cat. No. O5362

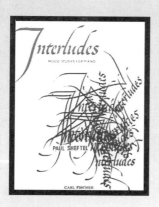

Cat. No. O4943

Cat. No. O5413

About Paul Sheftel...

Paul Sheftel is a nationally recognized leader in the area of keyboard stud-
ies; his numerous published materials are widely used throughout the coun-
try. In his role as educator, he has performed, lectured and conducted work-
shops in virtually every state in the US. He has been a pioneer in the creation
and development of instructional materials utilizing MIDI technology. His
software is in use nationwide as well as in many countries throughout Eu-
rope and Asia. He is currently composing electronic orchestrations to Carl
Fischer's "Music Pathways" piano course as well as for other books in the
Fischer catalog.

In addition to his private teaching studio in New York City, Paul Sheftel is
Adjunct Associate Professor at Hunter College, heads the undergraduate Piano
pedagogy program at the Manhattan School of Music, and has recently be-
come piano editor for Carl Fischer. He is also co-founder and director of
SoundStart Electronic Publications which has been developing MIDI-en-
hanced software for several music publishers.